Aging in Place

AGING
IN
PLACE

Navigating the Maze
of Long-Term Care

MARY MASHBURN

NEW YORK

LONDON • NASHVILLE • MELBOURNE • VANCOUVER

Aging in Place

Navigating the Maze of Long-Term Care

Published in New York, New York, by Morgan James Publishing in partnership with Difference Press. Morgan James is a trademark of Morgan James, LLC. www.MorganJamesPublishing.com

The Morgan James Speakers Group can bring authors to your live event. For more information or to book an event visit The Morgan James Speakers Group at www.TheMorganJamesSpeakersGroup.com.

ISBN 9781683509790 paperback
ISBN 9781683509806 eBook
Library of Congress Control Number: 2018934770

Cover and Interior Design by:
Chris Treccani
www.3dogcreative.net

In an effort to support local communities, raise awareness and funds, Morgan James Publishing donates a percentage of all book sales for the life of each book to Habitat for Humanity Peninsula and Greater Williamsburg.

Get involved today! Visit
www.MorganJamesBuilds.com

For Paul

"... The evil that men do lives after them;
The good is oft interred with their bones;"

~ *Julius Caesar* (Act III, Scene 2)

Table of Contents

Introduction

What motivated you to pick up this book and take a look at the inside?

Are you worried about your aging loved ones and what problems you may face in the future? Congratulations on your willingness to begin thinking about these issues and to look for solutions before a crisis happens. Many people "bury their heads in the sand" regarding these issues because it is easier to do that rather than engage in difficult conversations with loved ones. Let's face it. No one enjoys talking about what will happen when they are old and in failing health, let alone what their wishes for treatment and comfort would be if they are diagnosed to be in a terminal condition. If more people were willing to communicate with their loved ones concerning these issues and do appropriate planning before the "zero hour," their relatives would not be left scratching their heads and wondering if the decisions they are looking at making are really what their loved ones would have wanted.

Maybe your family is already in crisis, with one or more older family members hospitalized, and many serious decisions regarding medical treatment and long-term care needing to be made immediately. Carving out some time from your crisis- and deadline-driven schedule to read this book will give you some important insights into the difficult and often frightening issues you and your family are facing – and may even offer you some possible solutions that you have not considered.

In order to keep the language of this book as simple and direct as possible, I am going to refer to your aging loved one or relative as "she" or "her" (since, in many cases, that person really will be female) and designate her as your mother – which is particularly appropriate since, in many cases, your mother is the last surviving parent. Indeed, many of you reading this book are at wit's end trying to figure out exactly what topics you and your mother need to discuss; what decisions she, you, or both of you need to make; and where you both should look to find the extra support you need to carry out these decisions.

Discussing what your mother's wishes are if she is facing a life-threatening medical condition is just the first step. Figuring out what to do and what your mom wants should she become disabled – either with physical problems or dementia or both – is a bigger and usually more of a long-term problem. Open communication about these issues is never pleasant, but is absolutely necessary if you and your siblings are to discover your mother's wishes and provide the best care possible for her in accordance with those wishes.

You may feel that the prospect of you and your siblings opening up and discussing your thoughts and feelings concerning your mother's health and other topics discussed later in this book sounds much easier than attempting to discuss these issues with your mother and getting her to let down her guard and speak honestly concerning her wishes. Not only might she want to avoid talking about these difficult subjects altogether, she could very well think you don't know what you are talking about and can't understand what she is feeling. In addition, she may be very reluctant to discuss or allow you to help with financial matters because she absolutely does not think you are capable of understanding her financial situation. She may think that you "don't have a head for business," or that you couldn't possibly understand the complex system of Medicare and her other health insurance. Often (especially if dementia is already setting in and she is showing the signs of paranoia that often accompany the disease), she may feel increasingly vulnerable and be reluctant to discuss financial matters with you or allow you to assist her because she fears that you may take advantage of her and cause her to lose some or all of her hard-earned money.

Frequently, although not always, one sibling (is that you?) steps up to the plate and tries to talk to a parent about these difficult issues and has some measure of success because of trust that has developed over the years. While that is great, other problems can develop when the jealousies and hurt feelings of other siblings surface. Again, if a family addresses these issues as a group while your mother is still in relatively good health and has a relatively clear mind, much can be resolved with clarity and without bitterness. This book will guide you through the process.

As I stated above, many older people find it much easier to avoid discussing these issues with their loved ones and to avoid taking action to sign documents giving authority for others to act in their stead (powers of attorney, living wills, advanced directives, etc.). You are facing both short-term and long-term issues that often require quick decisions and action, and your mother may or may not have signed any of the important documents that would allow you to act on her behalf. So, besides worrying about all of the above issues, if you discover that your mother is permanently impaired to the extent that she may not in the foreseeable future be able to make decisions or handle financial affairs, then you and your family will in all likelihood need to start a court proceeding to establish a guardianship or conservatorship (the name depends upon the laws of the state in which your loved one resides). In addition, if your mother will need long-term care (nursing home or assisted living) for more than just the very short period which Medicare covers and does not have sufficient cash resources, someone will need to begin the intense and degrading process of applying for Medicaid on her behalf in order to cover the expenses of care – which typically will range from $5,000 to $15,000 per month, depending on her state of residence and the level of care she requires.

Ideally, whether you and your mother are attempting to plan for the future or you are in a crisis situation, you need to seek assistance from a variety of sources including an attorney, financial advisor, geriatric care manager, or social worker. I realize that in a true time crunch this is not always possible, but I cannot overemphasize the importance of getting good advice from a variety of professionals from several different disciplines in order that your mother and all members of your family will have the best insight possible into the various situations you are facing. Reading this book will give you insight into different issues you should consider and the questions you should ask in planning for the future with your mother as well as offering information and possible solutions if you and your family are currently facing the need to make important medical decisions for her.

The problems and issues I address in this book are not the kind for which you can find a truly happy solution. I cannot offer you a magic wand to wave and restore your mother to a younger and healthier version of herself. No one wants to deal with a loved one's failing health and memory. It is a cruel reminder of what lies ahead for each of us as we age.

Instead of magic, I offer you this: My hope for you after you finish reading this book is that you have acquired a real understanding of the problems you and your mother are facing, both now and in the future, and have a clearer understanding of the different sources of help and support available to you, both private and public. Even more importantly, I hope that your mother, you, and your other family members are able to use the information contained in this book to make decisions involving her care which will give all of you peace and strength as you face these challenges together.

When you are facing these daunting situations, it is important to have confidence in the person or team with whom you are working. With that in mind, the next chapter shares the journey my husband, attorney John Mashburn, and I took to acquire the knowledge and experience we needed in this area so we could express the compassion we feel for family members, caregivers, and older persons.

Chapter One:

"TEAM MASHBURN" – THE BACK STORY

I am a paralegal who has worked with my husband, John Mashburn, in his law practice in the village (now just barely a city) of Groveport, Ohio, located about twelve miles from downtown Columbus, since he opened his office in 1978. During that time, the scope of his practice evolved from a general focus to one that specialized primarily in probate and estate planning as well as real estate law. As his reputation as a probate lawyer continued to grow, he began receiving referrals from the court as well as from his clients. In the spring of 1988, one of the court magistrates invited him to join a panel of attorneys who would be assigned referrals for guardianships from the newly established Franklin County Adult Protective Services agency. For each referral he accepted, he would be responsible for determining whether applying for guardianship would be appropriate. Because that is such a serious step, Ohio law has established an application process that requires that the proposed ward (physically or mentally incompetent person) and that person's next of kin (who are residents of the state) be served with notice of the hearing on the application of the person asking to be appointed guardian. After the hearing (assuming that the court appointed him to be the guardian), John would begin the process of determining what would be the best course of treatment for the person's medical issues and what would be the safest and least restrictive living arrangement for the person. In addition, he would need to locate and reregister the person's assets (bank accounts, real estate, automobiles, stock) and income (usually social security and pensions) in the name of the guardianship. If the person's assets and income put him or her above the poverty level, John would be paid for his services from that person's assets (after receiving approval from the court for his fees). If the person had no assets and little income, then he would bill the county monthly for his fees (at a greatly reduced hourly rate). Most of the cases he accepted fell into the latter category.

His first case was Ellen, a widow who lived in her own home about five miles from our office. She suffered from dementia, was not caring for herself properly, and was extremely combative. She had one sister who wanted to be somewhat involved, but not enough to want to be appointed guardian. At that time, placement in a nursing home seemed to be the only course of action (There are a few more options now.). Working with the Adult Protective Services case manager (a licensed social worker), we found a suitable nursing home with an administrator who agreed to send a van and help us coax her into it. Luckily, Ellen had sufficient savings that she could afford to pay for her nursing home expenses privately, at least for the several months it would take until we could complete the guardianship land sale proceeding and find a buyer to purchase her house. Continuing to live in a nursing home, she fought the progression of her Alzheimer's disease (and the nursing home staff on bath days), and eventually passed away. Like many long-term nursing home residents, Ellen did not outlive her money. During the last two years of her life, she was qualified as a Medicaid recipient. In other words, the state required John to pay all but $40 of her monthly income towards her nursing home expenses. In turn, the state of Ohio, using a combination of Federal and state funds, would pay the difference of her nursing home expenses (based on a state compensation formula) and all of her medical expenses not covered by Medicare. Before she ran out of funds, however, we made arrangements for John to work with her sister to select and purchase an irrevocable prepaid funeral plan at a funeral home her sister selected. Unfortunately, when Ellen's condition deteriorated to a point at which we could have asked her physician to make a hospice referral, the Medicare hospice benefit was still in its infancy and very limited. Had we been able to enroll her in a hospice program as they exist today, she could have benefited from the extra care and attention hospice programs provide for several months before her passing.

Much has changed since John became Ellen's guardian in 1988, both in our office caseload and in the services available to older persons. John is currently the guardian of over 190 persons, some of whom suffer from severe mental illness or developmental disabilities, as well as those who are elderly and infirm. For the past four years, Crystal Davis, a licensed social worker with experience working with older individuals both in nursing homes and in the community as an employee of the Franklin County, Ohio, Adult Protective Services Agency, has been a part of our team, as well as other paraprofessionals who help manage the volume of paperwork and arrangements that must be made in handling such a diverse group of individuals.

In addition to the guardianship side of the practice, John continues to practice in the areas of estate planning and Medicaid planning, as well as in the administration of probate estates and real estate. Just recently, we have begun easing into the slow process of retirement with a little more speed than expected as John has entered into a partnership with Steve McGann, an attorney with several years of legal and guardianship experience, who also has a compassionate soul in dealing with persons facing these types of situations. Because I feel it would be a shame for John and me to retire completely when we have so much to offer to help others, I wrote this book with the goal of using our wealth of experience to provide insight and information to families of aging parents who are looking for solutions in helping their parents live as safely and independently as possible and in navigating the often complicated and confusing long-term care system.

Now that you know more about John's and my experience and ideas, I would like to share with you in the next chapter the stories of two of our dear friends, Florence Karpowicz and Pat Howard. Rather than going into detail about the many issues families face when trying to do the right thing for an aging family member, I believe that reading their stories will give you confidence in understanding that not only do we know what to do, but we are sensitive to your feelings of helplessness and desperation as you face a road full of obstacles in your journey through the maze of long-term care.

Chapter Two:

FLO AND PATTY JO

◆◆━━━━━━━━━━━━━━━◆◆

Over the years, John (along with the assistance of his faithful staff) has served as guardian or held power of attorney for nearly 2,000 people, as well as helping countless other families in taking care of their aging or impaired loved one; however, in nearly every case, John and I never knew the persons that we have cared for before their conditions deteriorated. We did not feel the heartache that family and friends experience as they helplessly watch their loved ones deteriorate physically and mentally. The exceptions were the cases of our dear friends, Florence Karpowicz and Patricia Howard. Because of the love I have for these wonderful women, their families have given their wholehearted support to my sharing their stories.

Florence and I met in 1976 in conjunction with my first job in a law firm and immediately became fast friends and partners in crime. Until the last few years, she was a bright, interesting individual whose greatest pleasure was giving of herself to others. She thrived in her profession as a legal secretary to Harold Wonnell, a brilliant and flamboyant Columbus trial lawyer, and dearly loved her husband Joe, her sons, and later her grandchildren. She worked for Mr. Wonnell until his death in 1999 and continued to work for his wife, Nancy, also an attorney, for more than a year until she retired at 75 to care for Joe, who was then suffering from Alzheimer's disease.

After Joe's death in 2001, Flo was at first disconsolate and blamed herself for allowing her children to persuade her to place Joe in a nursing home during his final months. In time, however, she began enjoying life again and actively pursued her many interests and socialized with her family and many friends. She called me her "intellectual friend," and we made many trips to independent movies as well as to the opera and plays. She thoroughly enjoyed accompanying us when we visited our daughter, Sarah, in London during her college semester abroad, and several years later was delighted to spend my birthday weekend with Sarah and me on a whirlwind trip to New York City. She also enjoyed other trips with family and friends, most notably a trip to Poland, the childhood home of both of her parents.

In her mid-80s, Florence began to suffer from mini-strokes, which resulted in a permanent and untreatable vertigo. She felt extremely dizzy and unsteady and very seldom left her home. She was often isolated for days at a time and lost weight as a result of a decreased appetite. I stopped to see her at least once a week and called her every day to give her "human contact." She insisted that she wanted to remain in her home as long as possible, but was resistant to having anyone come in to help her. I agreed that I would support her in this wish as long as I could. One fall Friday night, I found her in such a weakened state that she could not get up from the sofa to go to the bathroom. Worried that she might possibly need hospitalization, I urged her to call her son Joe whose wife, Gabi, is a nurse. She reluctantly agreed. Joe and Gabi came over immediately and moved her into their home that night. In the process of collecting her things, we discovered that besides being malnourished, she had not been managing her medications correctly and had not bathed properly in some time.

Fortunately, besides her will, Flo had already executed a Financial Durable Power of Attorney, a Living Will, and a Durable Power of Attorney for Health Care (all standard Ohio documents that permitted her sons to handle her affairs). Since Joe and Gabi would be her primary caregivers, they met with John and me to discuss Medicaid planning. They were interested in preserving the house for sentimental reasons because their parents had lived there since their marriage in 1949. At the time, Ohio law stipulated that if an immediate family member provided primary care for the patient for at least two years prior to admission in a nursing home, then the individual is permitted to deed his or her home to the caregiver. In addition, there is a five year lookback (aka penalty) period on any gifts made to third parties.

Accordingly, we prepared a deed transferring Florence's home to her two sons and recorded it immediately after she signed it. In addition, I urged Joe to begin the process of cashing in Flo's paid-up life insurance policies and using the proceeds to pay for an irrevocable pre-need funeral plan. Understandably, Joe took his time with this step as it is never easy to make funeral arrangements for a loved one even if that person is still alive.

For more than two years Joe and Gabi provided excellent care for Florence, whose health and memory deteriorated rapidly. I was so relieved that the vascular dementia did not rob Florence of all of her memory and that she still knew her family and me. Having any consequential conversations became nearly impossible, and the best way to talk with her was to tell her stories with the understanding that she might or might not comprehend. Because of the distance between our houses, I did not provide respite for Joe and Gabi as often as I would have liked, but many times I did stay with Flo so they could get away for an evening. It nearly broke my heart knowing that this once strong, capable, and articulate woman was totally dependent on others for all of the activities of daily living.

As I will discuss later, I am an advocate for early admission in hospice care. The earlier a patient enrolls in a hospice program, often the better his or her daily condition becomes. The extra support as well as the medication and equipment which hospice programs provide free of charge to patients and their families is invaluable. I had shared my views on this subject with Joe and Gabi many times and was not surprised when they enrolled Florence in hospice in 2015.

Because her condition still meets the criteria for enrollment in hospice, she continues to be a hospice patient, and I anticipate she will be in the program until she expires.

Several months after her enrollment in hospice, Joe and Gabi decided that because of her increasingly weakened state, they could no longer care for her in their home and placed her in the same nursing home where they had placed Gabi's mother some years earlier. I worked with Joe through the complicated process of applying for Medicaid, which I often compare to the most grueling and embarrassing physical examination one could experience. After much wrangling to get the approval of the transfer of the real estate, the worker approved the case.

My darling friend still survives as she approaches her 92nd birthday. She is a shell of herself, but there are moments of clarity. One morning I was showing her Facebook pictures of Ed, her other son, touring the old Chicago neighborhood with his oldest daughter. All of a sudden, Florence exclaimed, "That's my house!" I sobbed with joy at this flash of recognition. I treasure every infrequent return to her old self.

These moments are less and less frequent. Usually, our visits consist of my trying my best to engage Florence in some form of interaction since she rarely talks. Each time I see her, I wonder if that will be the last time she knows who I am. Nevertheless, I continue to live in hope that as Florence continues this process of "the long goodbye" that at some level she realizes that we who love her will stand by her side.

Pat Howard ("Patty Jo"), my friend and coworker for more than 15 years, found much satisfaction working in our office as an administrative assistant focusing solely on the guardianship side of the law practice. She prepared checks, reconciled accounts, coordinated the execution of forms, and spoke with persons under guardianship and their families with kindness and, when appropriate, with necessary firmness. This was Pat's "retirement job" as she retired from the Ohio State University Law School's alumni relations department with 30 years of service. Although she spoke fondly of her years at the law school, she truly enjoyed working with the diverse cast of characters for whom we were responsible and the interesting situations in which we sometimes found ourselves.

A lifelong smoker, Pat successfully stopped this habit for months at a time, only to start again when she decided that was the only way to cope with stress. In July, 1999, she stopped for good when she collapsed, was rushed to the hospital, and ended up connected to a ventilator for more than a week – no nicotine withdrawal symptoms in that method of quitting. She survived that incident and began a life revolving around oxygen tanks, breathing treatments, and expensive medications. Because she was so determined to continue working, I agreed to bring her work home. Daily I would schlep bills and correspondence to her, and we would chat about the cases as well as what was going on in our lives.

After about three months, oxygen tank in tow, she returned to work, and continued for nearly five more years until she retired again just before her seventieth birthday in 2004.

Pat and I continued to be close friends after her retirement. Despite her deteriorating medical condition, she returned to work on a very limited basis beginning in 2009. I thought she wanted to come back because she missed the stimulation of life at the office, but I later discovered that she really needed the extra money to pay her mounting medical bills. As her COPD symptoms worsened, she spent fewer and fewer hours working and had several short hospitalizations. Finally, in January, 2013, she left work for the last time in an ambulance after nearly collapsing from extreme difficulty in breathing.

Over the years of our friendship, I became acquainted with Pat's only daughter, Joan Killinger. Pat and I had often discussed the advantages and disadvantages of being an only child – no arguments or rivalries but no support. I assured Pat that if she ever got sick, I would be there for Joan all the way – and I was.

Like Florence, Pat had a Financial Power of Attorney, Living Will, and Durable Power of Attorney for Health Care in place; however, Joan had to face some real financial challenges and make several difficult financial decisions almost immediately, as Pat did not return home again after her January hospitalization, but spent her remaining days in a nursing home less than 30 minutes from Joan's home.

Besides facing the time-pressured process of finding an acceptable nursing home that had a vacancy, Joan also immediately had to begin the process of qualifying her mother for Medicaid and digging through her mother's paperwork in an attempt to find all of the necessary documentation. Although Pat was very much aware of the situation, she was too weak to be of much help. Luckily, one of Pat's friends from church was a member of the executive team of the corporation that owned the nursing home Joan selected. He assured Joan that Pat would be able to be in a private room as long as she remained in that nursing home even after Medicare ceased to pay her bill and she was a Medicaid patient. Even though that nursing home was more than a

30-minute drive from Groveport, I knew that would be the place where she would be most comfortable.

In assembling Pat's paperwork, Joan and I came to realize that because of her medical and pharmacy expenses, Pat was living on the edge financially prior to her hospitalization. The house was over-mortgaged, and her credit card debt and medical bills were significant. With two children in college, Joan had her own financial concerns and felt overwhelmed when faced with this situation. I explained to her that we would notify the creditors of Pat's medical situation, and they would write off the debts (What choice did they have?). I then informed her that she would need to liquidate the cash value in any of Pat's life insurance and use it to purchase an irrevocable funeral contract as well as any items that would make Pat's life in the nursing home more comfortable.

Since at that time all Medicaid applications involved face-to-face interviews and I was usually the lucky person from our office who attended these interviews, I have a positive relationship with many of the caseworkers and supervisors in the nursing home unit. In fact, when Pat had to apply for her mother's Medicaid when she was a nursing home resident, she got to meet one of our favorite workers, and he was assigned to the case. I also knew the worker assigned to Pat's case, and she worked as quickly as possible to get the case approved.

After the Medicaid case was approved, the biggest financial and logistical hurdle that Joan faced was the fact that because the house was over-mortgaged, there would in time be a foreclosure. She would need to begin the arduous process of going through all of her mother's things at the house she had lived in since her marriage to her second husband more than 30 years earlier. The task was even more difficult for Joan because she lived nearly an hour away from her mother's house in Groveport.

Once Pat grew stronger, she was both angry and accepting of her plight of being a nursing home resident. She understood that a nursing home was the only living arrangement that made sense for her in her condition, but she missed her independence and her friends. Sadly, many of the friends that she made in Groveport felt that the nursing home was too far away for them to visit frequently and complained that Joan should have picked a nursing home closer to them. In June, however, John and I brought her to an Eastern Star meeting where she visited with many of her friends and fought to outlast her exhausting excitement. None of us knew this would be her final trip to Groveport alive.

In the late summer of 2013, after consulting with the medical staff and me, Joan enrolled her life-weary mother in hospice. Many of the staff of what is now Kindred Hospice knew Pat from working with our office and strove to give her the best possible attention and alleviate as much of her discomfort as possible. As the fall wore on, Pat grew weaker and weaker and experienced more incidents of confusion and dementia as her oxygen-starved brain struggled to keep functioning. Finally, on the way back from family festivities, I received a call from Joan telling me that Pat had died on Thanksgiving afternoon, not too long after Joan and the family had left her side because she was too exhausted to participate in anything but a short holiday visit.

I miss Pat and her words of encouragement, which would buoy my spirit when I felt the situations I faced were impossible. The sweater she left behind when she exited the office for the last time remains on my chair as a reminder that she is still with me.

Chapter Three:

DIFFICULT CONVERSATIONS

◆◆━━━━━━━━━◆◆

Often people with aging parents come to our office looking for John and other members of our staff to serve as facilitators in difficult conversations they must have with their parents or loved ones. At some level, most of us are still children (even if we are 75+) in our relationships with our parents or older loved ones. Add dementia, severe health problems, malnutrition, or mental illness into the mix, and disaster can often ensue. The following are only a few of the many issues that you and your family should discuss while your aging mother is still able to be an active participant. Ideally, all family members should be involved in the discussion – but you should encourage your mother to make her wishes known to whomever she can speak most freely.

One of the most necessary and often most difficult subjects to discuss is a person's preferences regarding treatment for a potentially life-threatening disease or condition (Advance Directives). In a perfect world, your mother will discuss her views with loved ones while she has a sound mind and is in relatively good health. Unfortunately, too often these conversations never occur until a crisis is at hand, and family members – although often not prepared and having no clear knowledge how their critically ill relative would want them to proceed – are forced to make split second decisions which they often discover are not exactly the ones that their loved one would have made. Serious illness is a topic most people find difficult to discuss as it reminds us of our own mortality and vulnerability. Lisa Newburger, LISW, a dynamic speaker and health and wellness educator, has created a card game called "Hearts2Hearts," which serves as a springboard for discussions on these challenging issues, and may be ordered from her very informative website, discussdirectives.com. While great tools for discussion, Lisa's website and products are heavily geared toward Ohio advance directive documents: the Living Will and the Ohio Durable Power of Attorney for Health Care.

The board and staff of Aging With Dignity, a US nonprofit corporation, offer the Five Wishes document as a means for individuals to communicate very specific guidelines for care and health care decision-making, as well as nominating the persons they wish to make these decisions if they are medically incapable of doing so themselves. Currently legally acceptable in 42 states and the District of Columbia, the form was developed with the assistance of the American Bar Association's Commission on Law and Aging and the input of many medical professionals. In the remaining states that have yet to enact this form as the way for their citizens to put their advanced directives in writing (Alabama, Indiana, Kansas, New Hampshire, Ohio, Oregon, Texas, and Utah), residents of these states are permitted to attach The Five Wishes document on the back of the signed state-approved form as a way of giving further direction concerning their advanced directives. I urge you to go to Aging with Dignity's website and examine the Five Wishes online form (www.agingwithdignity.org/five-wishes/five-wishes-online).

What exactly are the Five Wishes? In short, they are five documents contained in one relatively small booklet written in plain language that, when completed thoughtfully, allow individuals to express in detail their preferences for care and designation of what person or persons should be permitted to make medical decisions following the guidelines in the document should they ever be medically or mentally unable to make those decisions themselves. The first two often replace official legal documents, while the last three set forth specific requests and preferences for treatments and procedures to make them as comfortable as possible in their final days, and information that the signers want their loved ones to know. They are:

1. **The Person Who I Want to Make Care Decisions for Me When I Can't**: This

is actually a durable power of attorney for health care (durable meaning that it will still be effective if the person later becomes incompetent). In other words, the signer names a person or persons who will not only be able to make health care decisions but be permitted to review the signer's medical records and discuss medical information with doctors and other health care providers without violating any confidentiality laws.

2. **The Kind of Medical Treatment I Want or Don't Want:** This is a living will document that addresses in great detail and clear language the signer's preferences regarding how aggressively they want the medical team to proceed to keep them alive. Currently, in most states hospitals, nursing homes, and even EMT teams follow the instructions for care (code status) that persons, or their designated representatives, have made in writing. Medical professionals often instruct persons who have signed advanced directive documents to tape a

copy to their refrigerators so that EMT teams
may have ready access to them and are able
to follow their instructions for care. In this
"lawsuit happy" era, nearly every physician or
medical professional performing emergency
treatment will initiate every lifesaving
treatment possible unless a properly signed
state-approved advance directive document
is in the patient's chart or readily available in
the patient's home (in the case of EMTs).

3. **How Comfortable I Want to Be:** This
    section allows the signer to set forth in as
    much detail as possible what methods of
    treatment to ease pain and increase comfort
    they want to be used in the event that,
    for whatever reason, they are unable to
    communicate instructions at the time. It also
    allows a person to ask for specific personal
    care treatments like warm baths, soft music,
    massage with oil, etc.

4. **How I Want People to Treat Me**: What
    a great opportunity this section provides in

giving a person the opportunity to describe exactly what they wish family and friends to do to provide the most physical and emotional comfort! It details many possible comfort procedures such as playing soft music, offering prayers, having loved ones' pictures at the bedside, etc.

5. **What I Want My Loved Ones to Know:** This final section deals with personal ideas and wishes rather than medical treatment. It also allows the signer to inform loved ones about funeral preferences. One of the kindest gifts a person with a terminal condition can give loved ones is communication concerning their feelings about entering into this stage of life as well as sharing their preferences regarding funeral arrangements. In fact, I know some people who have given their children the gift of choosing their funeral arrangements and prepaying them. Even though this can seem like a "creepy" thing to do (especially picking out a casket), I can tell you with absolute certainty that every

person I have talked with whose parents did this prior to their deaths were so relieved that they did not have to make the arrangements without any guidance or scramble around trying to pay the funeral director.

While discussions about advanced directives are critical in order to determine what a person's wishes are, it is often far more difficult to find out what your mother's wishes would be if the day ever came that she could no longer live independently at home. Many people are determined to remain in their own homes as long as possible, notwithstanding the problems of isolation, poor nutrition, hoarding, misuse of medication, etc. Others want to minimize the burden on their children and loved ones and cooperate with varying degrees of reluctance.

What if your family (with the important exception of your mother) unanimously decides that that it is absolutely not appropriate for her to remain living at home alone because her dementia has significantly worsened and her staying alone for any length of time puts her at risk? This very scenario happens quite frequently. Even if your mother has given you a power of attorney, she does not have to follow your instructions if you are asking her to do something she really does not want to do. Short of filing for a guardianship of the person – which would only upset your mother even more – a better alternative is to ask an experienced geriatric social worker to talk to her one-on-one about the situation and attempt to get her to try out the new living situation for just one night. This is often all it takes for a lonely woman to experience comfort and regular companionship again and conveniently forget her desire to return home.

The story of Jessie Louise Mashburn, John's mother, and how at the young age of 91 she made the decision that she could not return to her home after hip surgery, clearly illustrates what an uphill climb you could be facing. Jessie was a "hillbilly woman with a fiercely independent spirit." That independent spirit proved to be quite a challenge for her children and their spouses as she entered her 90s and grew increasingly frail. After falling twice at home in less than a month, she ended up in the hospital with a broken hip and was released to a nursing home for rehabilitation; but John and I both knew that returning to her little house – owned by my sister-in-law and her husband – was definitely not an option. To say that Jessie was not happy at the nursing home is a massive understatement. She made every effort to induce guilt in her two remaining children. Luckily for Jessie, who could not possibly have afforded any other option, John and I negotiated a workable price at our friend Pam Landis's board and care home. Pam, John, and our social worker, Crystal Davis, went to visit Jessie at the nursing home in Xenia and, not surprisingly, met with much resistance. Imagine our shock the next day when John's sister Kathy called and told us that Jessie was ready to move to Pam's! Thus began an eight month journey of laughter, tears, occasional battles of wills, cancer, hospitalizations, and finally Jessie's death after what I believe was the happiest period of her life since the death of her husband in 1992.

Whether your mother is able to remain at home or she decides that moving to a facility that will provide her the care she needs is the best idea, the support of family caregivers is a necessary element to assure a successful experience. Whether living across the street or across the country, the more family members who are willing to share their lives and their time with her, the greater the chance that she will have the highest quality of life possible during these years of change.

Another difficult topic of conversation is how your loved ones intend to dispose of a lifetime of possessions and mementos when the time to downsize, either by choice or out of necessity, arrives. This is truly a subject that no one takes any real joy in tackling, but avoiding the discussion can often have an unnecessarily severe impact on family unity. By the time they reach their seventies, many people have amassed quite a collection of possessions and mementos which have unique meanings to different family members who often hold quite different opinions as to the monetary or sentimental values of certain items. In this era in which "decluttering" is the buzzword of the day, many people encourage their loved ones to "simplify their lives" and get rid of items which may have little to no monetary value but which are truly precious to the person for sentimental reasons. Conversely, often family members will begin asking for various items which hold sentimental value to most or all family members long before their aging relative is willing to part with them. The resulting conflicts concerning the disposition of possessions often result in feelings of bitterness and jealousy among family members that may linger for years and may never be fully resolved. Many older people suffer unnecessary grief as they stand by helplessly and watch their children bicker about who gets what item without giving any thought to what their parents actually want. "After all," many of them rationalize, "Mom has no place to put that item any more, and I know she wanted me to have it." Additionally, some people have so many possessions that both they and their family members are overwhelmed at the process of leaving them or liquidating them and later suffer "purger's remorse" when they regret what they threw away in the haste of getting everything out of their parents' current residence in order to meet some type of deadline, self-imposed or otherwise. Although stressful, planning ahead for the placement of your mother's possessions can save time, money, and relationships.

Older adults and their children also have difficulties in discussing finances and estate planning issues. Usually, there is one sibling who takes the lead in these discussions, and parents often assume the roles of children as their offspring attempt to sift through their finances, giving them very little opportunity for input in making their own financial decisions. Sometimes this process of "taking charge" is truly necessary when failing health and memories occur. In many cases, however, the older adults simply need some additional time and explanation to understand their financial affairs and make the proper decisions. Working with ethical financial planners who specialize in the needs of seniors is often very helpful, reducing stress on both the older adults and their family members, and often giving new insight to all parties on different ways to meet their financial objectives. There are more and more financial planners who are Certified Senior Advisors and have been trained not only in discussing financial products helpful to seniors, but in approaching their clients with a manner of respect and patience that will put both the individuals and their family members at ease.

Finally, as I discussed briefly earlier, many adult children have absolutely no idea what their parents wish to have done at the time of their deaths. While more and more people are opting for the less traditional (and often less costly) alternative of cremation, many older adults still wish to have a traditional funeral complete with burial in a cemetery – no matter what the expense. In contrast, without knowing what their loved one's wishes are, many people overspend on elaborate funerals that would cause their thrifty parents to cringe (if they were still around), a practice which John calls "guilt spending." Let me repeat with emphasis – two of the greatest gifts that parents can give their children are specific instructions as to the burial and funeral wishes and a plan for payment. In contrast, one of the saddest events that can occur is a funeral for a Medicaid recipient who resides in a nursing home and does not have sufficient funds to pay for the burial that their family wanted. Our experiences in that type of situation are varied; some cities or counties have established "indigent burial funds" which permit funeral directors to bill the local government (subject to very specific guidelines) for a simple cremation or burial for persons who have absolutely no assets (usually nursing home residents who are on Medicaid and have spent their monthly allowances on cigarettes or other personal needs). In other cases, the nursing home owners will pay for an immediate cremation.

Another situation that can occur is illustrated in the story of Greta, one of the persons for whom John served as guardian and who has been deceased for many years. Greta was a vivacious and flirtatious Swedish lady with absolutely no short-term memory who lived into her late 90s, but she was in her late 80s when the Court appointed John as her guardian. For reasons we never discovered, she was estranged from her only son, but a fellow church member named Marguerite had made Greta her special project and over the years developed a real affection for her. Even though Marguerite cared for Greta, she did not want to accept the responsibility of being her guardian nor to be the person who had to remove Greta from her apartment because the dementia from which Greta suffered had made it impossible for her to continue living alone. After her placement in a nursing home, we sold the items that she could not keep in her room as well as some small pieces of jewelry and used the money to buy clothing and other personal items for her, as well as paying some of her bills. We asked Marguerite if she thought we should upgrade Greta's funeral arrangements with any of this money, but she assured us that Greta had previously purchased a prepaid funeral plan that carried out all of her wishes. We had no reason to doubt this as Marguerite then presented us with Greta's burial outfit and asked that we store it until the time came to use it. When, at 98 years of age, Greta's tired body finally wore out, we were able to handle all of her arrangements by telephone because Greta had already made all of her selections with ample funds in place to pay for them. Imagine how horrible we felt when we discovered that this woman for whom appearance was everything was being viewed at the funeral home in a cardboard casket painted to look like a metal one! Had we known this was the case, we would have upgraded the prepaid funeral to include an inexpensive metal casket. Life is full of ironies! Your take away from this story should be that if extra funds become available, one should at least take a few minutes to review the prepaid funeral and make sure everything is in order, despite others' assurances that everything is just as it should be.

Chapter Four:

ESTATE PLANNING

With the help of an attorney and the encouragement of her family, your mother needs to make sure that she has two types of estate planning documents in place: (a) documents that give direction with regard to her affairs while she is still living – Living Will, Health Care Power of Attorney (incorporating the Five Wishes), and Financial Power of Attorney; and (b) documents that give direction to family members and fiduciaries to handle her affairs after she passes away – wills, trusts, and other estate planning documents.

While all of these documents are important, the health care documents are extremely necessary so that your mom can make her wishes for medical care and treatment known and can name the person or persons she wishes to make medical decisions for her if she is unable to do so. Please look back at the preceding chapter for a detailed description of these documents.

Do you and your mom speak freely about her finances, or does she hold this information "close to the vest?" If she is not willing to be open about her finances at this point, she may or may not be willing to sign a Financial Power of Attorney document in which she names you or another trusted person to "act as her legal twin" and manage some or all of her financial affairs. You should reassure your mother that just because she is signing a power of attorney document, you are not required to handle her affairs just yet. Instead, you can agree not to use the document until such time as she needs help managing her finances.

Since you know your relationship with your mother, you may decide whether or not to tell her that if she does not sign these documents and name someone to act in her behalf to make health care and financial decisions for her, it could possibly result in the necessity of having a court-appointed guardian chosen for her, which may be a family member or may be an independent professional guardian with no knowledge of her and her wishes.

Why do people end up with court-appointed guardians? Some persons fail to sign these documents before they become physically or mentally unable to sign, either because they are not comfortable with naming a family member to handle these decisions or because they are unwilling to give up control. In other cases, family members decide that they do not want to serve even though they sincerely care about their loved one. For various reasons, they are unable or unwilling to make the difficult decisions concerning their placement and care and would welcome having an independent professional making these decisions.

The second category of documents is typically what most people think of when they talk about estate planning. Wills are documents that express a person's wishes for the distribution of his or her property after death and that name an executor to pay any outstanding bills and handle the distribution of their assets according to the terms set forth in the will. Trusts are agreements between a grantor (the person who owns the assets that are to be transferred to the trust) and a trustee (the person designated to manage and distribute the assets of the trust).

Setting up a trust not only gives a person the ability to establish an estate plan that, if properly implemented, will allow assets to pass directly to heirs without going through the probate process, it permits the grantor (the person who establishes the trust and whose assets are its subject matter) to set restrictions on the method and timing of distribution of assets. For example, if your mom wishes to give a certain amount of money or percentage of her estate to a minor grandchild but wants to distribute the money a little at a time, or wants it to be used for educational expenses, in the trust document she can instruct her trustee to do just that. If she plans early enough, she also could use a trust to protect all or part of her assets from being used to pay for her care should she require nursing home care later on. She should only do that type of estate planning with an attorney specializing in elder law as the federal rules concerning these trusts are very precise and change frequently in regards to these usually private documents that are not subject to court scrutiny.

Wills only govern the distribution of assets that must pass through the probate process. Unlike a trust, a will is only a private document until you die, when it becomes a matter of public record after it is filed with your local probate court. When clients come into our office to discuss estate planning, they are most concerned with how to keep their assets from being tied up in the probate process after they die. In addition, they are often reluctant to spend the money necessary to set up a trust.

There are also other ways to avoid probate besides creating a trust and transferring assets into it. Besides transferring ownership of your assets to a trust, you may pass any asset to an heir or heirs and avoid the probate process by naming beneficiaries on the forms provided by the financial institution. Any assets (bank accounts, stocks, and even real estate and automobiles in many states) that are registered in the name of an individual with the words "transfer on death to" or "payable on death to" are not subject to the probate process and are distributed to the beneficiary or beneficiaries. If your mom is willing to speak freely about finances with you, you should encourage her to check with her bank and financial advisor to review in what name or names each account is registered and what beneficiaries (if any) are listed. Then she can make the necessary changes to the beneficiary designations, if needed. This is a very important procedure to follow at the death of a spouse or other co-owner of an account. Often the staff at banks or other financial institution do not take the time to discuss adding a new beneficiary when they are working with the beneficiary of someone who has passed away to transfer the account or asset into the his or her name. It is particularly important to check on the beneficiary status of retirement accounts (IRAs, 401(k) plans and 403(b) plans) as there are immediate tax consequences if these assets must pass through probate because the account listed no named beneficiaries. If the owner of the account had designated a beneficiary, then that person may spread the tax liability over a number of years based on the age of the beneficiary.

Speaking about the importance of naming beneficiaries properly, I recall one expression I have heard many times over the years which often sends chills down my spine: "I know that if I put (name of one of several children) as the beneficiary on my (bank account, life insurance policy, IRA, etc.), she knows how I want the money to be divided and will take the responsibility to do the right thing." Unless there is actually only one beneficiary, that is a bad idea. Even if the child receiving the funds intends to follow her parent's wishes, life intervenes. Spousal pressures (and sometimes divorce), financial crises, illness, and even the death of the beneficiary before the funds can be distributed are all reasons why that person may be unwilling or unable to follow the plan. The safest way to insure that any account or life insurance policy is distributed the way you want it to be is to spell out your wishes clearly when you complete the beneficiary form with the bank or financial institution.

Which type of estate planning is better? Like the answers to so many of life's important questions, it depends. I am sure that you have seen attorneys who market "estate planning packages" which include wills, trusts, and advance directives all in a tidy preprinted notebook. While those are great for the right people, we have seen many grieving families bringing those notebooks into our office only to discover that after discussing the deceased person's family structure and finances, that person could easily have avoided probate without spending the money for such a comprehensive plan. Older people who are motivated to do estate planning often equate complicated and expensive with doing what is best, regardless of whether or not there is a less costly alternative that is just as effective in meeting their wishes and goals. The best advice I can give you is, if at all possible, take the time to seek out legal and financial advisors whose primary goals are to propose estate plans that are in the best interests of their clients based on their individual financial and personal circumstances.

So, what does that mean for your mom and her family? Every family chooses to communicate, or fails to communicate, about estate planning differently. Some people are very secretive about their wills and related documents and absolutely do not want their children to look at their wills prior to their deaths.

Others have a polar opposite opinion. They include their children in the trips to the attorney's office and painstakingly organize their financial documents so that their children will have no trouble closing out their affairs when the time comes. Most fall in the middle of these two scenarios.

Attempting to start the conversation with your mom can be tricky. Remember to start the conversation gently and give her enough room to preserve her dignity and independence to decide how much she wants to reveal to you. With love and respect, ask her if she would share with you the location of any wills or other important papers so that you might know what to do if something happens unexpectedly. She might surprise you and begin showing you these documents (and more) right away. If she seems reluctant to talk about these matters with you directly, share this information with her, and then encourage her to see her attorney to make certain that her legal documents are up to date and to see her banker and financial advisor to review the beneficiary designations on each of her accounts. She may welcome your accompanying her. Going through this process with her will strengthen the bonds of love and trust between you, since you were good enough to be patient enough to wait until she was truly ready to discuss these issues with you. If she resists your efforts to talk with her, do not force the issue. Instead, gently approach her again in a few weeks. If she is still resistant, don't give up; just continue attempting to bring up these issues respectfully and lovingly every few months. More than likely, in time she will decide to open up to you. She may decide not to share all of the details with you, but if she will at least let you know whether or not she has a will and some or all of the other documents discussed above and where they are located, then both of you will have at least some level of peace. Your mother will feel secure in the knowledge that she is retaining her privacy and has shared what she has determined to be important with you. And you will know how you can respect her wishes.

Chapter Five:

ACTING AS A FIDUCIARY

————◆◆————————————◆◆————

A fiduciary is a person who acts in a trusted capacity to protect and manage the assets and safety of another. There are two types of fiduciaries – health care fiduciaries and financial fiduciaries. Earlier, I discussed the roles and responsibilities of health care fiduciaries in my discussion of health care powers of attorney and the Five Wishes. Persons who act through health care powers of attorney are considered to be fiduciaries, as they act in the place of another to make health care decisions for that person. In addition, persons appointed by courts to serve as guardians of the person of individuals determined by courts to be unable to make health care and placement decisions for themselves act as health care fiduciaries, and are accountable to both the family and the court for their decisions.

Health care fiduciaries serve important roles, as the decisions they make directly impact the health and welfare of the persons in their care. People who need health care fiduciaries to make decisions are often very vulnerable and medically fragile. Their medical professionals and family members look to the health care fiduciaries to make sound medical and placement decisions to maximize each person's quality of life. They often work with physicians, health care providers, and family caregivers to obtain the information necessary to make decisions that will be the most beneficial for the person in their care. While health care fiduciaries are usually family members, independent fiduciaries often are able to work with family members to establish a family consensus on treatment plans and living arrangements that are in the best interest of both the individual and their relationships with other family members.

If you serve as a health care power of attorney or guardian of the person for your mother, you must keep the original power of attorney document or a sealed copy of the court order naming you as guardian of her person; health care fiduciaries are constantly required to show documentation before they sign consents for treatment or before they can get any health care information concerning the care and placement decisions they are required to make. In addition, HIPPA (Health Information Privacy Protection Act) laws often complicate the process of allowing guardians or powers of attorney access to pertinent medical information. Finally, even though health care fiduciaries may act without the consent of family members, as a concerned and responsible fiduciary you should make every effort to build a consensus for health care decisions among your siblings so that they may present a united front in discussions with the treatment team and the patients themselves.

Financial fiduciaries serve as either powers of attorney or guardians for individuals. In addition, many financial advisors are encouraging people to hold their assets in the name of a trust that they have created with the help of an attorney. In many of these trust agreements, the creator of the trust also serves as the trustee as long as they are able or desire to serve. While both these fiduciary relationships involve a high level of trust and responsibility, persons serving as financial powers of attorney and trustees are accountable primarily to the individuals and their families for their expenditures and investments, while guardians are accountable to probate courts and the rules that each court establishes. In most states, guardians must post a fiduciary bond as an added safety measure to ensure that they are investing and expending funds properly and safely. Despite the recent news stories written about guardians and powers of attorney who take advantage of the persons in their care and steal thousands of dollars, most people who act as fiduciaries – whether they are professionals or family members – do their best to be good stewards of the money and other assets for which they are responsible. (Take a look at the stories on www.aaapg.net.) If you act as a power of attorney, guardian, or trustee for your mother, you may face frequent scrutiny from bankers and other financial professionals who will repeatedly require and demand documentation before funds can be liquidated or transferred. In addition, you will often be required to provide several types of documentation in order to get the approval necessary to conduct business on her behalf. Be prepared to have your patience tested to its limit, but I sincerely believe that your motivation to do what is best for your mother will get you through any frustration you endure in the process.

Chapter Six:

NEW LIVING ARRANGEMENTS – AND HOW TO PAY FOR THEM

◆◆━━━━━━━━━━━━━━━◆◆

When the time arrives when your mother begins to face the limitations that go hand in hand with aging, one of the first questions she will probably ask is, "How will my life be changing?" Depending on the state of her health and her finances, there are many answers to that question. The following are types of places into which your mother could move when she feels that being at home is no longer an option for her.

Living with Relatives

While this is often not the ideal situation, many children want to make a real effort to try to take care of an aging parent. If this option is one that you or one of your siblings want to try, you should consider some of the following:

- Are you able to provide the personal and medical care your mother needs? If she has trouble walking, transferring from bed to chair, or needs help with toileting or bathing, are you willing and able to help her? Often local agencies on aging can send out case managers to assess your mother's needs and provide necessary equipment and arrange for assistance with personal care and home health at reduced rates (depending on your mother's financial situation). If she is financially able, you can work with home health agencies to send in workers to provide personal care and manage her medical needs (set up medications, wound care, etc.).

- How much time are you willing or able to devote to her care? Members of the "sandwich generation" are torn among responsibilities to children, spouses, and parents. Do not feel that you are in this alone. Your mother would probably welcome frequent outings to the senior center, particularly if she is still high functioning. Interaction with peers is a great way for her to feel a sense of purpose and community and is much better than her spending hours at home alone while you are working. If she is too frail to participate in senior center activities without supervision, then perhaps you should consider enrolling her in an adult daycare program which provides many activities and field trips, as well as offering personal care and medication administration. Beyond those alternatives, you should speak candidly with your siblings about stepping up to do their share in caring for your mom. Finally, you can work with your mother to hire home care agencies and private duty care providers to work in tandem with you to see that her needs for safety, medical care, and personal care are met.

- Are your immediate family members willing to adjust to this new situation? Adding another person to your household, no matter how warm your relationship, can often be stressful. Asking your spouse and children for their support and acknowledging the sacrifices each of them will be making are important first steps in making this move a success.

- Have you worked out the financial component of this arrangement? Most older people are more than willing to do their part to share in the payment of household expenses and the cost of any extra care. In addition, you should at least discuss with your mother how she wishes to compensate you for taking care of her. Being responsible for her care is a huge undertaking, and you may be pleasantly surprised to learn that she understands that you should be compensated for your efforts. If both of you agree, then it is very important to enter into a formal caregiver contract outlining any payment arrangements you and your mother have made. You should use the services of an elder law attorney to draw up this agreement in order to make sure that it meets state standards to preserve your mother's eligibility for Medicaid should there come a time when her condition deteriorates to a level that you will no longer be able to care for her in your home.

Once you and your mother (with input from your family) have come up with a workable plan for incorporating her into your immediate family group, then all of you can begin a period that could have been entirely full of overwhelming responsibility and frustration with a well-earned feeling of satisfaction that you have done everything you could to meet your mother's needs in her advancing years.

HUD Housing

Seniors whose annual incomes do not exceed 50% of the average annual income in the area may have an opportunity to stay in a HUD Section 202 Supportive Housing for the Elderly community in which residents pay a fixed percentage of their incomes for rent rather than a specified monthly amount. These senior living communities provide social activities, community meals, vans for transportation to shopping and appointments, and health and wellness programs, all of which promote better health, good nutrition, and increased socialization, with the ultimate goal of having residents remaining in the community as long as possible rather than being placed in nursing homes. Because there are usually long waiting lists for vacancies in these communities, you should encourage your mother to begin the application process to get on the lists of those communities that interest her long before she plans to move if she is interested in this type of housing and her income and assets meet the requirements. Moving to one of these buildings may be the best option your mother may have for maintaining her independence and enjoying activities and a social life while living within her limited income.

Continuing Care Residential Communities (CCRCs)

Usually developed by religious or fraternal organizations, these communities are designed to meet the changing medical needs of seniors who enter as independent living residents, but later may easily move into an area of the community that provides more care (assisted living or nursing home), either on a temporary or permanent basis. Designed to be a positive step toward attaining the goal of "aging in place," these facilities typically offer spacious and well-appointed apartments, restaurant-style meals, classes, activities, and social gatherings for their independent living and assisted living residents; and state of the art medical care and therapies, as well as appropriate activities, for those living in the nursing home area. Moving to one of these communities could be a great decision for your mother if she has sufficient assets to pay the monthly fees as well as a large endowment or entrance fee which many, but not all, of them require. Particularly if she has many interests and enjoys socializing, moving to one of these communities could actually improve the quality of her life by giving her life a renewed sense of purpose and allowing her to continue enjoying her relationships with her children and grandchildren rather than depending on some or all of them to take care of her. The downside of this living arrangement is, of course, the cost. Many seniors cannot afford this type of housing, but those who can are often able to enjoy their lives as actively and independently as possible with assistance from staff when it is needed.

Private Board and Care Homes

These are small group homes in which the residents or their families pay privately for care with the goal that they remain living there as long as medically possible. Owned and managed by nurses, social workers, or very experienced caregivers, these homes offer individualized care in a family-style environment to persons who, for a variety of reasons, can no longer live alone. You and your mom should consider choosing this type of living arrangement if she requires a lot of assistance in managing her daily routine and enjoys being in a small group environment. Unfortunately, these homes – which often provide excellent care – are in extremely short supply and seldom have vacancies. If, however, you find one that does have an opening, you should investigate it carefully and ask for references from family members of both present and prior residents since government regulation of these homes is virtually non-existent.

Assisted Living Facilities

These are primarily for people who require assistance with some of their activities of daily living (bathing, dressing, eating, managing medication, etc.) and often suffer from the beginning stages of dementia. Since most residents have at least some medical and/or mobility problem, these buildings, although often designed and decorated to look warm and inviting, are unmistakably medical facilities complete with nurse's stations, charts, and staff attired in medical uniforms. While some states provide Medicaid coverage for assisted living care, currently a very high percentage of residents pay privately for their care. Most assisted living facilities charge a basic daily rate and then assess monthly fees for progressively higher care needs. If your mother needs assistance with personal care and has some medical needs, you should work with her to investigate which assisted living facility would make her feel most comfortable. Unfortunately, when the time for such a decision arrives, your mother may be in a weakened state in a hospital or a nursing home, and you and your siblings must forge ahead to find a place that will meet your mother's needs at a cost she can afford.

Extended Care Facilities (Nursing Homes)

Providing the highest level of medical care for their patients, the executives of many nursing homes are reinventing these facilities that provide primarily short-term post-hospitalization care and physical and occupational therapy paid for primarily by Medicare and supplemental insurance for persons recently released from the hospital who are not yet ready to go home. Nonetheless, many facilities continue to provide primary care for persons suffering from the last stages of terminal diseases, chronic disabilities, advanced dementia, and Alzheimer's disease.

Should your mother require nursing home care, either for short-term rehabilitation or for long-term care, the most important advice I can give you is to show up as often as possible; and, if something does not seem right, question the staff immediately. Nurses and aides at nursing homes are often overworked and drowning in a sea of paperwork mandated by Federal regulations. In addition, while most of them are very caring individuals, they simply don't have time to answer their patient's constant demands for assistance as quickly as either the patients, their families, or even they themselves would prefer. Because "the squeaky wheel gets the grease," patients who have frequent visits from family members who take an active interest in their treatment receive more timely and consistent care than those who have few or no visitors.

After determining what the best care plan for your mother is, the next step is figuring out how to pay for it. In an interview with financial guru Suzie Orman for Next Avenue, Shelly Snelling has written an extremely readable article offering solid information on both the costs and challenges of paying for and providing long-term care and sage advice about purchasing long term care insurance: www.nextavenue.org/suze-ormans-advice-managing-long-term-care-costs. Ms. Orman's impetus for acquiring knowledge in these areas was her experience in caring for her mother and the financial and emotional challenges she encountered in the process.

As I discussed above, most of the options for care require a considerable cash outlay. A common and completely false "urban legend" is that Medicare pays for the entire cost of long-term care. Nothing could be further from the truth. As we discussed above, Medicare only pays for a very short stay (a maximum of 20 days at 100% and less than half of the daily cost for days 21 through 100). In addition, if your condition improves, if you reach your maximum potential in a physical therapy program, or if for some reason you can no longer participate in therapy, then Medicare evaluators will cut this benefit very quickly and require you to pay privately or prove immediately eligibility for Medicaid to pay the cost of any additional days you remain a patient at the nursing home.

Another way that some people pay for all or part of the cost of long-term care is to submit the claim to their long-term care insurance carrier. Traditional long-term care insurance operates like regular health insurance in that your condition must meet certain criteria set forth in your insurance contract before your claim is approved. In addition, the benefit is sent to you in the form of a check is based on a daily rate (usually adjusted for inflation) you established at the time you purchased the policy. Finally, once you qualify for payment, the benefit is only good for a definite period of time which you established when you purchased the policy (usually three to five years). The most important thing to remember about long-term care insurance is that you should purchase it long before you need it, as you must pass a medical eligibility test proving that you are in reasonably good health at the time of issuance.

In the last few years, several insurance carriers have been offering an alternative plan, a long-term care annuity which involves the purchase of an annuity that has a long-term care component, which allows the use of the value of the annuity to pay for long-term care. The primary advantages of these plans are that there are no health requirements and that there are no premiums to pay other than to set up the annuity. Lastly, if you never need long-term care, your beneficiary will receive the entire value of the policy plus any increase in value. If you or your mother are interested in this type of product, please consult your financial advisor to see if it is a viable option in her situation. For a more detailed explanation of this combination of insurance and investment products, please take a look at this Elder Law Answers article to gain a better understanding of long-term care annuities: https://www.elderlawanswers.com/long-term-care-hybrid-products-give-buyers-more-options-7812.

Also, if your father or mother served in the active duty military during any period of wartime, your mother may be eligible to receive a monthly benefit of over $1,100 per month through the Aid and Attendance Program offered by the Veteran's Administration. This link provides you with the V.A.'s official explanation of this program: www.benefits.va.gov/pensionandfiduciary/pension/aid_attendance_housebound.asp. She (or you on her behalf) must complete a lengthy and detailed application (bureaucracy beyond belief!) and wait an average of six to eight months before the benefit begins. While this amount alone does not entirely pay for any form of long-term care, it can provide your mother with funds to pay a significant part of the monthly cost of assisted living or home care. Should you decide to pursue this option, I recommend that you contact a financial professional to assist you. The good news about that is that professionals are prohibited from charging a fee for helping veterans or their families complete the forms. They do, however, attempt to sell you financial products or provide other services for which they are eligible to charge. Your local V.A. or agency on aging could provide you with some local referrals of professionals who could help you with this complex application process.

Finally, I will describe the most common way people pay for long term nursing home care – Medicaid. Medicaid is a need-based health insurance program for people who have very meager assets ($2,000.00 or less) and, except for nursing home residents, very low incomes. Because of the large dollar amount Medicaid pays for nursing home care for each eligible person every month, the application process is quite comprehensive and detailed, especially if the applicant is married. If you are acting on your mother's behalf in the process of filing a Medicaid application and you have the funds to spend, I urge you to contact an elder law attorney to counsel you through the process, which can be like running through a minefield.

I will only discuss the Medicaid application process and requirements for a single person, which is complicated enough for the purposes of this book. If your mom is married, the application process is even more daunting, and it is even more critical that she receives professional assistance from an Elder Law attorney. Go to http://www.nextavenue.org/what-couples-need-know-about-medicaid/ to read a short but thorough explanation on this complicated process.

The very first time that John and I assisted a married couple through the Medicaid application process in the early 1990s was for a couple I will call Bill and Irene. Bill and Irene lived in a trailer park just outside of Groveport. Bill had retired from the Air Force and was extremely devoted to Irene, who had developed Alzheimer's disease. Because Irene's illness was quite advanced, she was unable to sign a Durable Power of Attorney; so, John represented Bill in the process of applying to be her guardian through the Franklin County Probate Court. That all went very smoothly, but then we examined the assets. Years before, Bill got the idea that he wanted to make sure that Irene would have access to their savings immediately if anything were to happen to him; so, Irene opened a savings account in her name individually. They thought they had everything under control – not so! At that time the Medicaid rules mandated that a person must have only $1,500 in assets before he or she could be deemed eligible for Medicaid with no special rules or exceptions for married people. Had Bill and Irene owned that account ($85,000 balance at the time) jointly, the rules in effect at that time would have required that she spend $42,500 of that account rather than the whole balance.

The good news for Bill and Irene was that not too long after she was admitted to the nursing home, the rules changed thanks to the Spousal Impoverishment Protection Law. While this long-overdue legislation truly did prevent the "Community Spouse" (Medicaid buzzword for the healthy, non-institutionalized spouse) from losing nearly all of their assets to pay for long-term care for their ailing spouse, the bad news is that implementing this legislation caused the Medicaid application process for a married person to become devastatingly more complicated. Trust me – that is not an exaggeration.

Flash forward a couple of decades for an illustration of why representation during the Medicaid application process (especially for a married couple) is vital. Warren and Sharon were a couple in their 80s whom we knew, both personally and professionally, for more than 30 years. Then in his early 80s, Warren was suffering from prostate cancer and lung problems and was very weak. In addition, he suffered from severe depression and some other mental health issues that had only recently been diagnosed in a short stay at the "geri-psych" unit at one of our local mental hospitals. Sharon was completely at her wit's end during this process. Her husband of 60 years was probably dying, and his mental illness made him out of control. With reluctance, John applied to become his guardian and admitted him into a local nursing home. Before we even had a chance to initiate a Medicaid application, the overzealous manager of the nursing home's financial department had lassoed Sharon and taken her to the Medicaid office to complete an application for benefits. Please note that these people were not wealthy by any stretch of the imagination. While

John as guardian had access to Warren's funds, he did not have access to Sharon's. Despite my cautioning her otherwise, Sharon relied on the advice of the nursing home finance manager, resulting in the fact that Warren could not be approved for Medicaid soon enough to prevent a bill for one and a half months of private pay nursing care being issued. Sharon panicked. We advised her that the quickest way for her to stop the financial blood flow was to get Warren out of the nursing home, take him home, and enroll him in hospice to ease the burden for all involved.

Warren's stay in the nursing home was medically a great decision because the medical staff there had enough time to monitor the administration of the newly prescribed psychiatric drugs, which greatly decreased his symptoms. This change in his condition made it feasible for Sharon to take him home. Relying on extra care from her children and the hospice team, Sharon managed Warren's care at home until his death a few months later. John continued as Warren's guardian until his death, and worked closely with Sharon and the hospice team to provide Warren with the treatment he needed to have a peaceful and relatively pain-free existence in the months leading up to his death.

If you need to apply for Medicaid assistance for your mother in order for her to pay for her nursing home stay, you will need to provide the Medicaid worker assigned to your care with written verification of her income from the income provider and proof that her assets, including bank accounts, cash value of life insurance policies, investments, real estate (with the exception of her residence), and motor vehicles (with one motor vehicle being exempt) have a total value of less than $2,000 at the time of requested eligibility. In addition to meeting the asset test, the worker can ask for up to five years of bank statements in order to ascertain that no sizable gifts were made to third parties (including children) that could be defined to be improper transfers within such five year period. If she did transfer any significant sums ($1,000 or more) to anyone, she could be deemed ineligible for Medicaid for a time period dependent on the size of the gift or gifts, but not beginning until the date of the denial of the application. Because of the complicated nature of this process, if at all possible, I recommend that you employ an elder law attorney at least to review the facts of your mother's case and offer advice as to what to do to aid in getting the case through the process as quickly and efficiently as possible. Once you obtain approval on the case, however, your work is just beginning. Besides paying the monthly amount specified on the official Medicaid notice of approval of the case, which represents all of her income less any amounts paid for additional medical insurance and a small monthly personal allowance ($50 in Ohio), you must report any changes in her income or the receipt of any assets which make her ineligible for Medicaid, and complete and submit an annual Verification of Assets and Income form to the Medicaid worker assigned to her case.

I realize that this chapter gave you a lot of information to process and probably left you shaking your head and wondering how you and your mom will ever make the best decisions for her care and how to pay for it. In time, however, with the support of your family, your mother will comfortably settle in to whatever living situation makes the most sense for her. There will undoubtedly be days when she has no use for you and tries to make you feel that uprooting her and altering her routine were the worst things that have ever happened to her, but overall she will embrace her "new normal," and although you will wish that your "old mom" could return to be your biggest advocate and cheerleader, you will at least be relieved that she is safe and that you are able to take care of her and see that her needs are met.

Chapter Seven:

PUBLIC AND PRIVATE RESOURCES

◆◆━━━━━━━━━━◆◆

There are a variety of both public and private resources to which you and your family can reach out when attempting to find help for your mother, as well as gaining more knowledge into her condition and ideas for improving the quality of her life. You and your family are not alone in this journey. These professionals and agencies are able to work with both your mom and your family, whether in a crisis situation or in an attempt to make things easier for her to maintain as much normalcy as possible.

Adult Protective Services

Every state now has at least a small program that strives to protect the most vulnerable populations. As in the case of children's services departments, concerned friends and relatives may make anonymous referrals to these agencies, which will send social workers to the residence as soon as possible to investigate the situation and intervene quickly, if necessary. Often these investigations result in the local prosecutor issuing an emergency protection order.

Elder abuse of all types has become a more and more serious problem. I am sure that you have read many stories about persons preying on older persons and bilking them out of their life savings with the promise of a sizable return on their investments. In my experience, I have even seen older people willingly sign over their homes to others, often with a promise of some kind of long-term benefit, either financial or personal. When confronted with the facts, sometimes individuals will relent and return the real estate or other assets to the older person in order to attempt to save themselves from lawsuits or even criminal prosecution. Others, however, especially unscrupulous family members, will insist that there was no wrongdoing and even face criminal charges rather than admit they have taken advantage of these most vulnerable people.

Even more alarming are the stories of physical abuse and neglect by caregivers. Often older people deny any problems out of feelings of embarrassment or a sense of duty to protect the abuser, especially if they are a family member. In other cases, both parties suffer from some type of mental illness or cognitive impairment e.g. dementia), and physical neglect occurs because neither person can cope with the situation. John and I encountered such a situation when we received a referral from a local hospital concerning a female patient in the ICU who was suffering from extremely serious pressure sores. The EMTs, acting on a referral, broke into the house and discovered that the woman had been sitting in the same chair for several weeks without getting up, despite the fact that her adult son and only child, who obviously suffered from some type of mental impairment, lived in the home with her. Fortunately, the woman survived. After receiving several weeks of intense hospital treatment, she was ready for release from the hospital. By that time, the Court had appointed John to be her guardian, and he made arrangements to place her in a nursing home, since returning her to her clutter-filled home to live with her son was definitely not an option. She spent her remaining days in a nursing home with daily visits from her son who never did understand why his mother could not return home where he could care for her.

The most common type of elder abuse, however, is self-neglect. Many older people, particularly those suffering from dementia, gradually lose the ability or the desire to keep themselves clean or care for their medical problems to the point that they are putting their health and safety at risk. As you may already have experienced with your mother, older persons are often very resistant to suggestions or help from family members. Often, but certainly not always, they are more receptive to suggestions from strangers, particularly those whom they see as experts or authority figures (social workers, nurses, doctors, attorneys, etc.). In many cases, however, if you and your family members are able to work as a team with the help of professionals, you may greatly improve the quality of your mother's life, health, and safety, whether she remains in her own home or moves to another, safer environment. She may not appreciate your efforts at the time, but, more often than not, she will accept the changes and even be thankful that you had the courage to intervene.

Daisy, an octogenarian suffering from COPD and tied to her oxygen machine, lived alone in her home in north Columbus. The only home care she had was an aide who came in twice a day and helped her move around, assisted with toileting, and made certain that she had food for snacks in easy reach since Meals on Wheels delivered a hot noon meal daily. The rest of the time Daisy lived alone and never left her chair and her friend, the oxygen machine. Her nephew, Daisy's only next-of-kin, loved her and readily admitted that he could not "be the bad guy" and facilitate her admission to a nursing home – the only solution to provide her the best ongoing medical care for her based on her financial situation. When John applied to become her guardian, he asked for and received a quick hearing date. While we waited for a hearing, I worked with a nursing home and arranged for her admission the day after the guardianship hearing. That day, I hired a private ambulance to come to Daisy's home to transport her to the nursing home. Since we knew that she would not be willing to go, John and I met her nephew and the driver at the house. Daisy was absolutely furious! John and the ambulance driver persuaded an unhappy but physically weak Daisy to let them wheel her into the ambulance and transport her to what turned out to be her new home. In the next few days, Daisy calmed down and slowly began to enjoy being among people. She died several months later. At her sparsely attended funeral, her nephew (John's fellow pall bearer), again expressed his gratitude that his aunt was able to spend her last months in a safe environment.

Local Agencies on Aging

These organizations, funded by local and state taxes, also provide support to seniors and their caregivers. They often provide many in-home services at a reduced cost based on the recipient's income, such as Meals on Wheels, adult daycare, in-home personal care, and light housekeeping, and supplies (including alarm buttons) that allow seniors the ability to live independently in their own homes longer. In addition, they serve as a clearinghouse for information concerning many issues involving senior care and are a great resource to see what is available locally. They also often offer events and educational opportunities for seniors and their caregivers. I encourage you to contact your local office.

In Ohio and many other states, these agencies also administer a "waiver" program for seniors who – if not for the services provided by the program as a supplement to care provided by family caregivers – would have no alternative except to enter a nursing home for their care. Should she qualify, your mother would be eligible to receive many services without charge, including adult daycare (including transportation, if needed), supplies, medical equipment, the services of home health aides, housekeeping services, and assistance with medications. The "waiver" program in many states also has a program that pays for a stay in an assisted living facility provided that facility can meet the person's medical needs.

While I am sure you are thinking that the "waiver" program sounds like the answer to a prayer, your mother is only eligible for the program if she is on Medicaid. As I have described several times earlier, obtaining Medicaid eligibility for your mother is quite a procedure. If you think she does qualify and could really benefit from these services, then it is definitely worth the effort to apply for this program.

Alzheimer's Association

Your local chapter of the Alzheimer's Association can also be a valuable source of support and information. In addition, their website, www.alz. org, provides not only a wealth of information concerning research, new treatments, and helpful ideas for managing behaviors and other symptoms but also links to the websites for local chapters. Local chapters of the association offer many educational opportunities for families and friends, local resources for care and treatment, and often have their own programs for respite and adult daycare. Even if your mother does not suffer from dementia of the

Alzheimer's type, this organization provides the same services and resources for individuals suffering from any type of dementia, their families, and caregivers. I am quite confident that your checking in with your local chapter will give you many ideas for support as well as afford you various opportunities to increase your knowledge about the causes and treatments for all types of dementia.

Geriatric Care Managers and Geriatric Concierges

These caring professionals could provide greatly needed assistance to you and your mom in both devising and carrying out a care plan for her, particularly if you are trying to manage your mother's care from a distance, which is becoming more and more common. Geriatric care managers are nurses and social workers – with a number of years of experience assisting the senior population – who work with you in forming a plan to keep your mother safe and as healthy as possible while living in her own home. In addition, they often accompany her to doctor's appointments and can communicate with both you and the doctor concerning her care. This is particularly helpful if you and your mother live many miles from one another. It is a great comfort to know that even though you were not able to be there, someone who could understand the doctor's instructions and information was at your mother's side. Geriatric concierges do have experience working with seniors without having the professional credentials of geriatric care managers. Their roles are to carry out the plans you and the geriatric care manager make by transporting and escorting your mother to and from medical appointments for physical therapy, podiatry, etc.; coordinating and providing care at home by way of fixing meals, shopping, errands, arranging for repairs and cleaning; and other tasks that make your mother's life at home more manageable. Both geriatric care managers and geriatric concierges are paid privately for their services. If, however, your mom has long-term care insurance and has been approved to receive in-home care services under the policy, the cost of their services could be partially or completely covered.

Because of the fact that currently in Ohio there is no way for persons without long-term care insurance or private funds to use a geriatric care manager,

John could use Marcia Wool, LSW, our geriatric care manager of choice, only in cases in which the person had the funds to pay for this important service. As illustrated in the following story, when the person could afford her services, the support and knowledge she provided were invaluable.

George and Martha, a husband and wife who had significant assets, were both very ill octogenarians who were determined to remain at home at all costs (or not exactly "at all costs" because they did not want to spend any money to pay for home care). George was very supportive of John's becoming Martha's guardian because he was too ill even to attempt to try to continue to take care of her himself. He even conceded that Martha should go to a nursing home. We had other ideas. Because George and Martha had well over $100,000 in savings and one of our favorite board and care facilities had a vacancy, we arranged for Martha to be transported there after a brief stay in the nursing home. Now semi-retired, the owner of the board and care home, whose name is also Mary, specialized in caring for bedridden individuals, and in her care, Martha's condition slowly improved. Although George was actually happy that Martha was receiving superior care, he remained adamant that he was going to continue to reside in his own home.

As George's physical and mental condition deteriorated, we were able to obtain a doctor's statement that George was so ill that he needed a guardian. The Court appointed John to be his guardian quite soon, and immediately we began working with Marcia and Mary to coordinate a plan to reunite him with his wife. On the appointed day, John, Marcia, Mary, and I all met the ambulance at George's home, and the five of us (including the ambulance driver) began the process of "selling ice to an Eskimo" and trying to convince him that he needed to allow the ambulance driver and his associates to load him into the van and reunite him with his wife. It was indeed a five-person team effort that could not have been accomplished without Marcia's professional skill. George was one angry man that day. Later that day, George and Martha were thrilled to be reunited and spent the next several months at Mary's until Martha's death. George spent nearly another year at Mary's until his tired heart gave out, and he joined Martha.

National Guardianship Association

This association offers many educational programs, both live and on their website, for family members caring for their loved ones. Their website, www.guardianship.com, offers information on a variety of topics regarding care of persons who can no longer care for themselves. It also offers continuing education and certification programs for both professional and family guardians and provides a nationwide list of Certified Guardians and Master Guardians and their contact information. This organization advocates for the rights of individuals not able to care or make decisions for themselves to have as much input as possible into the decisions regarding their care and living arrangements that their guardians make on their behalf.

Society of Certified Senior Advisors

Founded in 1997, this organization, www.csa.us, educates and certifies financial, legal, home care, and other service providers who strive to care for seniors and their families. These professionals have all received special training, been tested in their knowledge, and are attuned to the special needs of seniors and their families. Their website provides a list of their certified professionals in order to aid you in finding a professional who has been specifically trained and certified in working with seniors in your area. It is very important for your mother to work with professionals whom she trusts and who treat her with the dignity and respect she deserves.

National Academy of Elder Lawyers and Elder Counsel

Members of these two groups are elder law attorneys who have received additional training in issues facing seniors and their families, and offer creative solutions to complex problems facing seniors, particularly in the areas of Medicaid planning and estate planning. They are skilled in sitting down with your mother (and her family members, if she wants them to be included in the meeting) to discuss her wishes, offer her explanations to her questions, and present creative financial solutions that could possibly allow her at her death to pass more of her money to her heirs rather than spending it on long-term care while she is living. While typically they work with people who have significant savings, they often offer free consultations which could give your mother and her family important insights.

After reading my description of the Medicaid system – in which I made a real effort not to go into too much detail and really frighten you – you can really understand why having a creative legal mind working with you and your family in this process can be a real asset. John and I have gone to many Medicaid planning continuing education events, including a week at the Elder Counsel Institute event in San Diego, and have spent countless hours with eyes glazed over as expert attorneys speak in painstaking detail about the updates in Medicaid regulations, both at the state and local levels, and spew forth acronyms (SPLIMPA, PAM, CSRA, etc.) faster than we can locate and read their meanings in the written materials they provide. My description of Medicaid planning and the Medicaid application process as "finding one's way through a giant maze with just the right touch of indignity thrown in" should be enough to persuade you that you should seek counsel sooner rather than later in preparing for your mother's possible trek down this road.

Chapter Eight:

Hospice – the Beginning of the End or the End of the Beginning

————◆◆————————◆◆————

Hospice is a word that stirs emotions of fear and despair in many of us. We look at it as a time of preparing for the end of life. Many of us believe it is a program designed to serve the needs of someone at the very end of their life. Nothing could be further from the truth. Instead, hospice is a service for persons suffering from serious medical conditions, and provides healing care for both patients and their families in their inevitable journey.

Hospice agencies provide supportive medical care as well as emotional and spiritual support in either home or nursing home settings, at no cost to the patient as medical insurance, either public (Medicare or Medicaid) or private, pays for the entire cost of the service, provided that the primary doctor and the medical staff of the hospice company agree that the patient's condition falls within the Federal medical guidelines for hospice enrollment. In fact, many people find that their medical costs (particularly the cost of prescription drugs) actually decrease or disappear totally as the hospice benefit pays 100% of the cost of prescription drugs prescribed for the care of the primary diagnosis as well as for all treatments to relieve pain. In addition, the hospice benefit pays for equipment and supplies – such as hospital beds, special mattresses to help prevent bed sores, etc. – to allow the patient to return home in comfort and safety whenever possible or to provide additional comfort for nursing home hospice patients. Finally, if the patient is living at home or with a family member, the hospice company may arrange for a few days of respite for the exhausted caregiver by paying for the patient to stay in either a hospice facility or a nursing home.

Your mother may have many good years ahead of her despite her advancing years and the medical problems that accompany aging. As her medical condition changes, it is very important to continue the conversation with her about her wishes concerning how aggressively she wants her medical team to treat her condition. Using the tools of the Five Wishes and the other advanced directives described earlier is certainly the best way to get a clear understanding of her wishes; however, if she has balked at signing any documents or even discussing these important issues, as is often the case, then you and your other family members must band together to make these important decisions as the next of kin. Hospice programs provide very beneficial medical, social work, and spiritual resources to help your mom and her family do just that.

The media often portrays people suffering from cancer, ALS, or other terminal diseases as the most common group using hospice services. While it is true that these persons do often enroll in the program, many elders who suffer from any type of dementia which results in a general decline of overall health and weight loss may easily qualify for hospice services. In addition, if your mother is suffering from chronic conditions such as emphysema, COPD, or the complications of diabetes, and her condition meets the medical criteria for hospice, both she and her family could benefit from hospice enrollment.

Previously I listed some of the services that hospice provides. Many people mistakenly believe that this service provides 24 hour in-home care. It does not. Hospice workers that provide personal care (bathing, massage, wound care, etc.) typically visit a patient in the home or nursing home two to three times a week, as do social workers and clergy. Nurses and doctors visit at least weekly but are always available in the event of a crisis or if pain becomes unmanageable.

Even with the support and assistance of a hospice service, caring for a critically ill person at home is an often overwhelming responsibility that you may or may not feel able to attempt. Whatever decision you and your family decide is best, you can rely on the support and advice of the hospice staff to help you make your mother as comfortable and dignified as possible during this difficult time. If you decide that caring for her in your or another sibling's home is not an option, placing her in an assisted living or nursing home is an alternative that you should select without feeling guilty – which is very much easier said than done.

Most children want to do whatever they can to make their parents comfortable and follow their wishes as they embark on their final journey, but many times for a variety of reasons, such as the adult child's physical inability to be a caregiver, that option is not possible. In those cases, working with a hospice service can provide both you and your mother with an extra level of care and support in a nursing home or assisted living setting. Not only will their medical staff discuss treatment and pain management options with you, their social workers and clergy will spend as much time as needed with your mom and your family members to make the transition from home to facility as smooth as possible. They share the goal that all involved will be at peace with the decision, and they are committed to giving your mother the best quality of life for whatever amount of time she has left.

A common expression used in healthcare is "continuity of care." The staff at many nursing homes and assisted living facilities is constantly changing and is often a combination of facility employees and temporary staff. While in most instances they are well-meaning and make every effort to provide good care, they often honestly claim that they do not have enough information to respond in sufficient detail when asked how your mother is doing when you call or visit the facility. They also are often so busy tending to the needs of their patients and completing the myriad of paperwork that Medicare and Medicaid require that they often can spend very little time with you discussing your mother's care and condition. In contrast, hospice staff is always available by phone to discuss her care with you and will send someone to see your mother at the facility as soon as possible if you have a concern about her condition.

Although hospice services are meant to be for persons who are expected to have no more than six months to live, often, as in the case of my friend Florence, people remain on the service for much longer periods of time. If the general slow and steady decline in health – and sometimes the dementia that often goes with it – are the symptoms which have made your mother eligible for hospice care, then she too may be a hospice patient for a considerable amount of time. In fact, several studies have shown that in many cases hospice or palliative care, rather than care with a goal of improving or curing the patient's condition, actually results in longer life spans. For more information on this phenomenon, I encourage you to read the research available on the National Hospice and Palliative Care Organization's website.

My favorite hospice story involves our dear Greta, whose funeral preplanning debacle you read about earlier. Greta was 98, in a nursing home, and failing fast. Her friend Marguerite and I met with the hospice social worker sent after her physician made the hospice referral and John had signed the necessary admission paperwork. It was very clear that Greta would no longer be with us the following month. What could we do with the limited funds that were in her personal account at the nursing home to make her life better while she was still with us?

When Greta was still able to engage in conversation (which she would promptly forget five minutes later), I discovered that she thrived on engaging with people, particularly good-looking men. Keeping that in mind, as her time on this side of the dirt grew shorter, I arranged for a schedule of bedside sitters, one of which was the very good-looking nephew of one of my friends. Which one of these people do you think was with Greta when she drew her last breath?

The peace your mother and your family can gain working with a hospice organization is often cumulative, and I encourage you not to be afraid to look into hospice enrollment if you note any marked decline in your mom's condition, rather than waiting until the last few days or weeks of her life to do so. While enrollment at any stage of a terminal condition is always very beneficial, a longer period of service, if indicated, can bring a higher quality of life and more physical comfort for your mom, as well as a greater level of acceptance and calm for your whole family. I understand that, in almost every case, discussing the subject of hospice enrollment for a loved one is a devastating event; however, the holistic care your mother and your whole family can receive upon enrollment is such a blessing that it is well worth enduring these painful conversations.

Our Family Can
Manage This on Our Own

This is the statement I often hear when people talk with me about their aging parents. Privacy, pride, and parsimony are the three excuses families use when they explain why they do not need help in managing their parent's legal, financial and medical affairs. "No one, especially my (insert appropriate family member), needs to know my business." As I mentioned in the beginning of the book, many seniors fiercely guard their privacy, often to their detriment, because they want to avoid any family conflict, they are fearful of being exploited, and, understandably, they are frightened of losing any of their independence and autonomy. Add into the mix the fact that many of them falsely believe that Medicare will pay their long-term care expenses, and they (if they are well enough) and their families are left scrambling when serious illness or dementia (or both) enters the picture.

"I am absolutely fine. My mind is sharp as a tack. I'm going to take care of myself until one morning I just don't wake up."

That could very well be the case – but what if it's not? An intense desire to continue to live as independently as possible without being a burden on anyone is a common aspiration among those over 65. Many of them who have faced problems caring for their parents or other family members realize the importance of planning ahead and "hoping for the best but expecting the worst." Others, however, stubbornly maintain that they are fine and talk about being set adrift on an iceberg if their health should deteriorate to the point that they need 24 hour care. That never happens. Families of people who embrace that attitude are left scrambling as they try to gather documents and financial information to prepare for a guardianship proceeding, all the while worrying how the long term care and hospital bills will be paid and realizing that they can forget the idea of inheriting the "pot of gold" that Dad had set aside for them.

"Those lawyers will rob me blind! You're so smart, son. Can't you get those forms on the internet that will get the job done for a lot less money? I don't have much money, but I do want my children to get the house."

This lament is more common than you would care to believe. Only education and exposure to attorneys sensitive to the concerns of seniors will put more people at ease so that they may feel comfortable enough to get their affairs in order so their families will be able to take care of their needs should there come a time when they cannot do so themselves, and if they plan well far enough ahead of time, they can be assured that they can leave a financial legacy to their family members and charities.

Conclusion:

THE JOURNEY OF A THOUSAND MILES

◆◆————————————◆◆

Whether you are reading this book because you were looking for answers in anticipation of what you may face someday, or because your family is in the midst of an elder care crisis, I hope you and your family now feel much more informed, better prepared, and ready to face the multitude of situations you will encounter, the decisions you will be forced to make, and the bureaucratic labyrinths through which you must wind your way as you strive to keep your mother as safe, happy, and healthy as possible. Henry Miller wrote, "One's destination is never a place, but a new way of seeing things." It is my wish that as you face and handle these challenges, often with every fiber of your existence being constantly tested, you will emerge a stronger and more compassionate person, ready to share your experiences with – and offer hope and inspiration to – others as they deal with their own painful realities with their aging loved ones.

In an effort to give you additional ongoing support at no cost, I invite you to join my private Facebook group, Mary's Caring Community, in which I hope you will gain further knowledge on various elder care and elder law issues as well as share your experiences with the group. I truly believe that experiential learning is a necessary component in the situations you are facing and that the benefit that others will gain from your sharing your stories is both precious and immeasurable.

Acknowledgments

This book would not have been possible without John Mashburn, the man I have loved with my whole being for nearly 41 years. His tireless dedication to the elderly, the mentally ill, and the developmentally disabled – and his kindness and fairness to his clients and friends – have earned him more respect than he will ever realize.

Our daughter, Sarah Vogel, also deserves a special word for her many years of patience as we tried to make a positive difference and do the right thing for those in John's care. Since she was barely five years old, she has been involved in many of our "missions of mercy." I am quite sure that she was not always a willing participant, but I am also certain that she has grown into a caring and compassionate woman at least in part as a result of her experiences with us. We are so proud of the wonderful person you have become!

I have learned so much from the many social workers, admissions staff, nurses, psychiatrists, hospice professionals, and direct care providers who often have thankless jobs caring for those who suffer from physical and mental disabilities as a result of the aging process, mental illness, and developmental disabilities. I would especially like to acknowledge Crystal Davis, LSW, and Pamela Landis (Zimmerman), LPN, with whom we have worked in one capacity or another for more than 25 years. These women served pivotal roles in improving the quality of life of so many people, including John's mother, the unforgettable Jessie Louise Mashburn. Her medical and social work professionals I would like to thank specifically are: Ann Downing, Jackie St. John, Marcia Wool, Linda Kay, Joanna Hughes, Andy Capehart, Ursel McElroy, Melanie Cooley, Bruce Tolbert , Kathy Peeples, Miriam Cox, Joan Rankin, Bill Brundage, Mary James, Dr. Michael Witter, Dr. Paul Harris, Jr., Dr. Paul Harris, III, Dr. Donald Friedenberg, Dr. David Turner, Dr. George Harding, the staff at Twin Valley

Behavioral Health, OSU Harding, Riverside Methodist Hospital, and NetCare Access, as well as the dedicated mental health workers who serve so many patients in Franklin County under the different agencies of the ADAMH board.

Besides John, I would like to mention in particular the fine work of other attorneys in Franklin County who have served many years as guardians, specifically Kevin Craine, Michael Juhola, Susan Wasserman, and others too numerous to mention, as well as the staff and magistrates of the Franklin County, Fairfield County, and Pickaway County Probate Courts.

Richard Tapps, Esq. and the Law Firm of Browning & Meyer also deserve a special thanks as Messrs. Tapps, Browning, and Meyer have all endured my convoluted questions concerning Medicaid planning, special needs trusts, and pooled trusts over the years.

To the Morgan James Publishing team: Special thanks to David Hancock, CEO & Founder for believing in me and my message. To my Author Relations Manager, Gayle West, thanks for making the process seamless and easy. Many more thanks to everyone else, but especially Jim Howard, Bethany Marshall, and Nickcole Watkins.

Finally, I would like to thank the teachers and professors who profoundly influenced my love of language, literature, and writing (and taught me to eschew the passive voice): Janet Detterman, Mary Smith Thomas, Cheryl Doebel, Dr. Frederick Lemke, Dr. Robert Joyce, Dr. Nancy Siferd, and Dr. Ruth Wahlstrom.

About the Author

Mary Mashburn, Certified Senior Advisor and paralegal, has spent more than 30 years working with seniors, persons suffering from ongoing mental illness, and developmentally challenged persons and their families in conjunction with the law office of John Mashburn in Groveport, Ohio. A graduate of Heidelberg University and the Capital University Law School, she divides her time between the law practice and her involvement in various civic, social and philanthropic activities.

Thank You

I appreciate so much the confidence you have shown in me by taking the time to read this book, and hope that you will take away more than a few ideas you can use in your own family's situation, either now or in the future. Now that you are aware of these issues and some of the resources that you can use, I would like to offer to you as a special "thank you" a complimentary telephone strategy session with me to discuss your individual situation and additional insight into possible solutions. Please email me at agingstrategieswithmary@gmail.com to schedule your session.

Morgan James
Speakers Group

⌁ www.TheMorganJamesSpeakersGroup.com

We connect Morgan James published
authors with live and online events
and audiences who will benefit
from their expertise.

Morgan James makes all of our titles available
through the Library for All Charity Organization.

www.LibraryForAll.org

Printed in the USA
CPSIA information can be obtained
at www.ICGtesting.com
JSHW082358140824
68134JS00020B/2137